Love

~ris book

Your October 1995

CW01509613

FRENCH RESISTANCE
IN SUSSEX

Barbara Bertram

FRENCH RESISTANCE
IN SUSSEX

Barbara Bertram

Barbara Bertram

BARNWORKS PUBLISHING
PULBOROUGH, ENGLAND

First published in 1995 in Great Britain by
Barnworks Publishing
Bury, Pulborough,
West Sussex RH200 1PA
Telephone: 01798 831410

British Library Cataloguing in Publication Data.
A catalogue record for this book is available from the British
Library.

Hardback edition: ISBN: 1-899174-01-X
Paperback edition: ISBN: 1-899174-02-8

Printed and bound by Redwood Books, Trowbridge, Wiltshire

**In memory of all my 'Hullabaloos'
who faced danger so courageously**

Lysander showing additional fuel tank between
wheels

Cartoon by Goyet

*Moon: "Oh dear, every month it's the same
shambles"*
Gendarme: "Hurry or I shall have to book you"

FOREWORD

by Group Captain Hugh Verity,
DSO*, DFC, RAF (Ret'd)

During the second World War a surprising
number of secret intelligence networks were built
up in occupied France. The agents sometimes
came to England by sea but many were picked up
on moonlight nights by Lysander or Hudson
aircraft of No.161 Squadron, Royal Air Force.
We landed on meadows in many regions of
France and brought them to Tangmere near
Chichester, where Major Anthony Bertram was
one of the escorting Officers who met our
passengers.

He would take them to his home at Bignor
under the South Downs in West Sussex where his
wife Barbara would welcome them, feed them at
four a.m. or at whatever time they arrived, and
give them beds. I am so delighted that this
charming account of her war, which she first
wrote some fifty years ago, can at last be
published. When some of us pick-up pilots from
Tangmere went to parties with her French guests
on nights when operations had been cancelled, we
greatly enjoyed meeting Tony Bertram's pretty
young wife. We had no idea of her truly arduous
and dedicated work, with no domestic help,

which she describes here with a great sense of humour.

Although many agents were dropped into France by parachute, we generally took some out on our pick-up operations. If these were delayed by forecasts of fog, Barbara's guests might stay at Bignor for several days and they had to be amused without anybody knowing what was going on. In looking after them and their morale, Barbara would get to know them well. Her vignettes of some of these exceptional individuals make fascinating reading.

This rivetting narrative of life inside a part of the Secret Service from the point of view of an attractive young mother will explain why 'Madame Barbara' was so much loved by some 200 gallant French men and women who were her guests.

Hugh Verity
Richmond, 1995

INTRODUCTION

by Anthony Bertram

On the 27th of January 1946, in the Cours d'Honneur des Invalides, the British Ambassador presented a Westland Lysander to the French Air Ministry. By this symbolic act the secrecy was lifted from a remarkable series of operations and a most personal and dramatic relationship between a group of British officers and the French Resistance.

This Lysander belonged to a Flight which, from October 1941 until the Liberation, had regularly landed in occupied France to establish the two-way traffic that was necessary to supplement the one-way traffic of the parachute.

We stood facing it in two groups, one was of the pilots, operators and passengers who had survived, many of them still haggard from torture and prison; the other of British officers who had organised these complex operations or trained the

French operators. Among them was my wife, whose part in the affair had been unique.

Between these groups and the aircraft there paraded, of course, the high-ranking officers and officials who are always so prominent on such occasions and so innocent of their significance. Flanking were detachments of the Royal Air Force, the Armée de l'Air and the Garde Républicaine, with bands and standards. In this way the gawky old aircraft, that had often rested on French soil for two or three minutes in an obscure field, was consigned for ever to a French museum, a pensioner among pensioners.

After the last flourish of trumpets and the march-past and when the generals had gone, the two groups mixed and went off to the celebrations which were to last for some of us until three o'clock in the morning. The aircraft was left in the drizzle, under the sagging cloud that recalled so many anxious days when the telephone announced "Operation Off" … "C'est off".

In the text which follows my wife describes one aspect of what lay behind this commonplace of ceremony and sentiment. My work between moons - for we lived by the moon - was to train some of the French who were responsible for finding fields, organizing operations at their end and finally carrying out the delicate task of controlling the landing of an aircraft at night with no help but pocket torches. During moons I looked after the outgoing and incoming passengers. As our house was within half an hour's drive of the operational aerodrome, it was natural to use it as a forward base for this work. The overwhelming importance of secrecy forced us to establish an elaborate 'cover'. The story was that we ran a hostel for French officers convalescing. There could be no servants on the premises at night and yet no sense of mystery. The village must not talk. This clandestine life added enormous complications to what was already a sufficiently complicated task for my wife, whose small house with four bedrooms was sometimes expected to accommodate up to twenty people.

That I think is enough preliminary explanation. Perhaps it can only be fully understood by the two hundred odd French men and women who passed through the house, the pilots and the handful of French and English officers whose duties put them into the secret.

Although I do not see that a man should necessarily be modest about his wife's work, I prefer to quote in its praise what has been written by a Frenchman more qualified to appreciate it. The following passage is by Rémy, one of the first heads of Resistance - the vintage of 1940 - and is reproduced by his permission from the first volume of his Memoirs, "Le Livre du Courage et de la Peur" (Edition aux Trois Couleurs. Paris 1946).

Huit jours plus tard je me rends sur ce même aérodrome d'où j'étais parti à la fin du mois du mars dernier. Les prévisions météorologiques sont mauvaises, l'operation est remise au lendemain. Nous allons passer la nuit dans une charmante maison des environs, qui appartient à une dame anglaise, Mrs Barbara Bertram, qui s'est proposée comme hôtesse des oiseaux de passage. Mrs Bertram deviendra immensément populaire auprès du tous les clandestins en instance de départ ou qui arrivent de France. Elle est très gaie, c'est une délicieuse maîtresse de maison qui fait tout elle-même, qui se lève très tôt, se couche la dernière, prend soin de ses hôtes, de ses deux enfants, de son poulailler, de son clapier, de la chèvre, de son jardin et trouve le moyen d'être constamment libre pour un bridge, ou pour un promenade, ou pour jouer au darts, ce jeu de fléchettes en honneur dans toute l'Angleterre…

Je n'envie pas l'existence de Mrs Bertram. Elle ne voit que quelques heures ceux qui arrivent de France (oh, les yeux qu'ils ouvrent devant les oeufs sur le plat de bacon, le lait crémeux, les pâtisseries) elle voit le plupart du temps pendant deux ou trois jours ceux qui doivent partir, mais ceux-ci sont des gens nerveux, impatients, irritables, angoissés, pour être franc. Elle réussit de telle sorte auprès de ces hôtes difficiles que j'ai souvent entendu dire "Le meilleur souvenir que nous avons emporté d'Angleterre a été celui du séjour forcé que nous avons fait chez Mrs Bertram" Elle a conquis le coeur et la reconnaissance de tous les Français qui sont passés chez elle et, j'en suis bien sûr, sans avoir jamais fait aucune allusion à leur mission - c'était là un sujet de conversation interdit sous son toit - elle a raffermi bien souvent le courage de plus d'un.

"A week later I went down to the same airfield from which I had taken off at the end of the previous March. The weather forecast was bad, and the operation was put off till the next day. Off we went to spend the night in a charming house near by, belonging to an English lady, Mrs Barbara Bertram who had volunteered to act as hostess to us birds of passage. Mrs Bertram was to become immensely popular with all the secret agents leaving for France or arriving back. A gay and delightful hostess, she did everything in the house herself, first up in the morning and last to bed at night, looking after her guests, her two children, her hens, her rabbits, the goat, and her garden, but always with time to spare for a hand of bridge, a walk, or that favourite diversion of the British, a game of darts...

"I didn't envy Mrs Bertram her life. She saw the people arriving from France for only a few hours (oh, how they gazed in amazement at the fried eggs and bacon, the creamy milk, the cakes). The ones who were leaving were mostly there for two or three days; but they were nervous, short tempered, impatient, and let's face it, scared stiff. Difficult guests, but so good was she with them that I have often heard them say 'Our best memory of England was the time we had to spend in Mrs Bertram's house'. She won the hearts and the gratitude of all the French who passed through it; and though I am sure that she never said a word about what they were doing - that subject, under her roof, was taboo - many left her with their courage renewed."

(Translation by Sir Robin Hooper, pilot)

Anthony Bertram
Bignor, 1946

MY INTRODUCTION

It is hard to believe that the events I wrote about took place over fifty years ago. In some ways it seems like yesterday. I can still visualize many of our 'Hullabaloos', as our small boys affectionately called the French because they 'chattered so much in an unintelligible language'. I can still feel the excitement, anxiety and love of those years. On the other hand, of course, there must be much I have forgotten and much I have muddled. Looking back, it sometimes seems a nightmare, drivers get jumbled up with one another, 'Hullabaloos' fuse together and one 'op.' melts into another. When I remember the strain and constant activity and noise it seems impossible that I loved the job so much but I was fifty years younger then. The fact that all the French men and women who passed through our house were under great strain and always conscious of the likelihood of being tortured, bound them to us with an intimacy and love that was very special and very personal.

I think of all that happened between the autumns of 1941 and 1944 in two ways. One factual, as far as I can remember being what really happened and the other what it felt like at the time. I recorded them both and then managed to interweave the two. I wrote this in 1946 when it was still fresh in my mind and going round and round in my head. My husband's Introduction was written at the same time.

I have not identified most people except by the name I remember them by: sometimes a Christian name, sometimes a nickname and sometimes a surname. Names meant so little to me as I knew that often they were not the person's real name anyway.

I should like to thank Mrs. Jane Carpenter for editing and co-ordinating my MS, written at various times between 1945 and 1975.

Barbara Bertram
Barnes, 1995

1

On clear nights moonlight sought out the tiny hamlets hidden in the folds of the hills. In one's imagination they might become enchanted places, safe places, far from the conflict or the fears that beset mankind.

In 1940, however, moonlight began to govern our way of life and brought the war, not merely into our lives but into our home.

At the beginning of the War we were living at the Manor in Bignor, under the South Downs in West Sussex. It is a stone-built Elizabethan manor house with the unusual feature of a small stone animal on each gable: a sign we were told, of the two male animals that a manor kept for the use of the village. It is rare as far east as Bignor but this feature used to be fairly common in the west, though none survive.

It was really a farm house but we rented only the house and garden. To the west is the church of the Holy Cross with two big yew trees, to the east the farm buildings including a large flint dove-cote later used as a creosote pit, and across two fields the Roman Villa that makes the little village of Bignor well-known to thousands. To the north there are fields dropping down to Bignor Brook and Bignor Park and to the south a glorious stretch of the Downs.

There was my husband, myself and our two small boys; Tim aged seven in 1941 and Nicky aged five. There was also Duff-the-dog, Peter-the-cat, Caroline-the-goat, two rabbits, about twelve hens and two hives of bees.

As I had two young boys I was not called up and was occupied with the voluntary work women did in 'safe areas' - collecting Blood Donors, W.V.S. work, evacuees and so on. This of course was not considered as work, just something to do with one's spare time.

My husband, Tony, had been in the 1914-18 war and was in the Officers' Emergency Reserve so, in 1940, he was called up to his old regiment, the York and Lancaster. As we lived in Sussex he applied to be transferred to the Royal Sussex Regiment - they transferred him to the Durham Light Infantry! As he was forty-three he was sent to the Depot at Brancepeth and there would have remained for the duration if a young subaltern had not written to his brother-in-law who was working at the War Office with the French, to say:

"There's an old chap here who speaks French fluently and who is bored at being stuck at the Depot. Can you use him?"

The first Tony knew of this was when he was summoned to the War Office. He reported in full fighting kit complete with canvas bucket, full of hope that he was being sent out somewhere. When he was told he was to work for MI-6 with the French he tried to get out of it. He told the officer interviewing him that he did not like all that lying. "Do you like all that killing?" the officer replied.

So he reluctantly agreed to do it but he was never reconciled to the life of deceit, though he was full of love and admiration for the French with whom he worked.

The interview did not take place actually at the War Office but at one of their secret hide-outs that no one was supposed to know about, although a great many did. I often had to go to one of them later on and I always found myself looking over my shoulder when I approached it, to make sure I was not being followed.

The first secret device Tony encountered was when he went to wash before lunch. The cold tap ran hot and the hot one cold. He turned to an elderly high-ranking officer standing next to him and said:

"I suppose that's to get us used to secrecy."

"I don't think that's funny, young man," was the reply.

He quickly learnt that a sense of humour was not appreciated.

So in the autumn of 1941 Tony went to London. His first job was to take a party of Frenchmen up to a place near Manchester for parachute training. As he was over forty they tried to persuade him not to jump himself but he insisted that he must do all that his men did. The preliminary training was very tough but he got through that and his first three jumps alright but on the fourth he landed badly and broke his pelvis. 'The Office', with true MI-6 subterfuge, rang me up and said he had broken his ankle.

When he returned to London they made him a Conducting Officer, whose job it was to escort the French while they were in England. One of the first things they asked him was whether he knew of a small house in West Sussex, not too far from Tangmere aerodrome, that they could use as a hide-out for French agents. He suggested our house, knowing I had had quite enough of evacuees and would welcome the chance to do something for the French.

I was sent for and had a very pleasant lunch, during which no mention was made of the house but as I left the officer who had entertained me said:

"I hear you are letting us use your house. Write and tell us what accommodation there is."

The house had four bedrooms, three large enough for two beds and one little single one. There was a fairly large drawing-room and a dining-room. I said I thought I could put up four or five. 'They' said that was splendid and would I give up all my other work and my evacuees and get ready. 'They' did not tell me what to get ready for. 'They' never told me anything ever. Of course I had to sign the Official Secrets Act and I am sure 'They' must have put MI-5 onto me.

I gave up my W.V.S. work and, with relief, got rid of my evacuees but I kept on Blood Donor collecting. Then I sat back and waited; nothing happened for three weeks.

The secluded position of the house in a tiny village and standing well back from the road up a typical farm entrance was ideal for a clandestine job but was far too small. The living rooms were fairly large but the kitchen was tiny and equipped only for a small family. There was only one bathroom and one loo. The three big bedrooms had running water but not the little room. The water supply was not too good. It was pumped up from a stream at the bottom of Bignor Hill. The stream was fed, in turn, by a spring. As we were the highest point of the village, we were the first to suffer if it went wrong. There was a weight on a string in the bathroom which told us if the water in our tank in the roof was getting low. One of my jobs was to keep an eye on this, especially when the house was full. If it showed dangerously low I would have to wait until after dark so as not to be seen by anyone on the farm. Then creep out to the huge pig sheds in the farm yard, with only a faint torch to prevent me from falling over the heavy chains that always seem to lie about in farm yards. There was an outside staircase attached to the pig shed, leading to a sort of attic. I had to grope my way along this attic to the middle where the water tank was and tie up the ball-cock while hundreds of pigs below me snored and grunted. Finally, I crept back knowing that, in an hour or two's time, I must go back and untie it for fear the farmer should discover in the morning what I had done. He considered his pigs more important than our French men.

The War Office rented the house for £5 a week, paid for all our food in the moon periods and gave me a wage of £2 a week. At the end, when we were moved to a far more expensive house in Bedfordshire, they increased this to £5 accordingly.

During the three weeks when nothing happened the village began to wonder why I was doing nothing and, above all, why I had no evacuees. Then without warning, at about seven o'clock one evening an English naval officer, John, turned up with three Frenchmen and a girl driver.

"We want dinner punctually at seven-thirty," he said.

"What on earth do you think I'm going to give you at a moment's notice?" I gasped.

"I don't know. That's your job," he replied, cheerfully.

That was the beginning. After that I knew that I had to be ready to feed any number at any time.

At this juncture I should explain that the moon was all important. So we lived by the moon; last moon or next moon instead of last month or next month.

During dinner that night, Tangmere rang up and said, "C'est off". This mystified me as I still had not been told what my job was all about. John and the driver went back to London the next morning leaving the three Frenchmen with me. They were Aimon, Justin and Michel. Aimon owned a chain of brothels in the south of France and when we went for a walk around Bedham, I found that Justin was intensely interested in geology and we spent a happy morning looking for fossils in an old gravel pit. Michel told me that he had been a prisoner of the Germans and made to work on a farm planting potatoes and that as they planted them, he and the other prisoners ground the potatoes with their heels to prevent them sprouting. I don't think I could have done that even to spite the Nazis. I never heard how he had escaped back to France. The next day I took them all up to London.

When at last Tony told me what we were up to, I discovered that we were working with the Intelligence Section of the French Resistance. Not S.O.E., the saboteurs, who went out to France to blow up bridges and later to fight in the Maquis but with men and women who went backwards and forwards from the autumn of 1941 to the Liberation of France in September 1944, getting information. We didn't drop them by parachute, we landed them in Occupied France at night. These very difficult and dangerous operations could only take place when there was a moon; during the second and third quarters.

When the job really got going, this is what happened. At the beginning of a moon period Tony or one of the other Conducting Officers would ring me up from London to say he was coming with three or with six or, occasionally, with nine. That meant three, six or nine French and for every three there was a Conducting Officer and a driver. Sometimes there were also high-up French or British officers or Tony's immediate superior, who we only knew as K.C. We soon had a 'Scrambler' fitted to the telephone, so that the operator at Sutton Post Office would not be able to understand the messages which came through.

I quickly found that my having said I could put up four or five meant nothing at all. We frequently put up eleven or twelve and sometimes as many as nineteen. Once, we put up twenty-one. That time, a strange male driver slept in the bathroom.

The usual drivers were wonderful girls. They were in the Motor Transport Corps and drove and maintained big Chryslers. They were chosen because they spoke French well or else were utterly unselfconscious about their school-girl French. As well as their official duties they were expected to amuse the French, which they did admirably. They also often helped me wash-up but they weren't supposed to. They were all young, some married and some already war-widows. Two of them married Conducting Officers. One of these got engaged in the middle of a big operation. She tried to play bridge with a letter proposing to her in her pocket and him ringing up every other minute for an answer. They were immensely popular with every one and must have made all the difference to the French waiting to go out.

The party would arrive from London at about three-thirty in the afternoon, punctual if Tony was bringing them and always late if it was John. We would have a cup of tea and then each of the French who were going out would have to search himself thoroughly to make sure he had nothing on him that would show he had been in England - no bus or cinema ticket or letter. This searching was very necessary and more and more care was taken over it but, even so, slips were occasionally made. One Frenchman was in the Metro in Paris one morning, standing in the usual squash of passengers, when he found that a copy of the previous day's Daily Telegraph was sticking out of his overcoat pocket. He waited until he was nearly at his station then he slipped it out of his own pocket and into the pocket of a German officer standing next to him and quickly got out. This was an oversight easily made as the searching took place in the drawing-room when the coats were hanging up in the hall. I am glad to say that Tony was not the Conducting Officer in charge that day. It was even thought dangerous for men to go out with hairs from our dog on their trousers, so a clothes brush always had to be handy for them to use at the last minute.

After they had searched themselves they gave up any British money they had on them. If there was a lot it was kept until their return but they generally put small change into a Red Cross collection box we kept handy or, if they had been with us for a day or so and met Tim and Nicky, they often gave it to them.

Then they were given a fake French identity card and a fake ration card and lots of French money - fake too for all I know. They were also given, if they wanted them, a revolver, a kind of cosh they could conceal up their sleeve and a thing that looked like a fountain pen but squirted tear-gas if you pressed a knob. They were always rather sceptical about these. One day, some of them let one off in the bathroom and shut the door and, without telling me what they had done, asked me to fetch something from the bathroom cupboard. My state, when I rejoined them in a fury with my eyes streaming, was enough to convince them that it was very effective!

They were also given imitation French cigarettes, matches and soap and a tooth brush, pocket comb and razor blades not marked "Made in England". At first I had to find these things, which was not easy. I did find unmarked tooth brushes once and bought twenty-four but it was too chancy and soon they were made especially for us. At first I had to keep all cakes of soap as soon as the name on them had worn off, for their use, but this was found to be dangerous. If used in a public lavatory it was noticeable that it lathered too well. So soap, also, was especially made almost as gritty and bad as war-time French soap. There was a difficulty about the imitation Gauloise: the gum used on the packet was too good so that it did not disintegrate as soon as opened, as the real ones did. This too was remedied.

As well as those provisions there were also tiny compasses, knives, pencils, magnifying glasses and cards printed in microscopic letters and maps printed on fine silk. All these things were kept in a secret cupboard. The study part of our drawing-room was book lined and before the war we had a coke stove there to supplement the open fire in the other part of the room. We noticed after a while the books over the stove were getting damaged by the heat so we removed them and covered the front of the empty shelves with a sheet of plywood on which we hung a picture. When a locked cupboard was necessary in the war, we simply detached the plywood, fitted a lock onto one of the shelves and there was a secret cupboard. The picture could be replaced by a dart board and the plywood made a good background for bad shots.

While this searching and giving out of things was going on, the drivers and I went through their luggage looking at everything they had bought whilst in Britain to see if it was marked "Made in England". If they had bought a new suit, the buckle on the back of the waistcoat had to be cut off and the straps sewn together, this generally had to be done while they were wearing them. Hats were confiscated, they are stamped on the leather band inside and you cannot remove that without making the hat too big. We had nine hats at the end of the war. Gloves had the button wrenched off. Shirts were easy. We rubbed the mark very hard with Milton and it either rubbed out the word, or it rubbed a hole in the shirt. Once I seized a pair of beautiful pink silk pyjamas and was just starting with the Milton when their owner snatched them from me: he had bought them in Paris before the war and refused to risk them being spoilt.

During this time of packing and re-packing I was often asked for all kinds of probable and improbable things. I had to be careful these were not marked too. I was asked for string, nails, boxes, bags and tins, for safety pins, hair pins, scissors. I got into the habit of hoarding everything in case someone should ask me for just that.

One day, between the arrival of a party from London and their departure for Tangmere, two other Frenchmen and a typist arrived. They borrowed our typewriter and worked in haste in the dining room while the rest had before-dinner drinks. I have no idea what it was all about or why they needed two steel knitting needles, which of course I didn't get back.

Then I had to do a horrible thing. They were going out to Occupied France and were going to be in great danger of being arrested and they knew that if they were, they would be tortured. Some of them felt that they wouldn't be able to withstand torture so, to prevent themselves giving away their friends, they asked me to sew a little tablet of poison into their cuff. "Greater love..."

When all this was done it was generally time for a drink before dinner. The time of dinner was fixed by Tangmere. One of the pilots would ring me up during the day to say what time they wanted them over there nine, nine-thirty or ten depending on the state of the moon, the time of year and how far down into France they were going. We fed them as well as we could and always ended with a tot of rum.

Then they would go off to Tangmere except the odd officer who stayed at Bignor. If they were late in starting for any reason, the drivers were allowed to use full head-lights and Tony was ordered to sit in front by her with a loaded revolver on his knee and if a policeman stopped them, he was to shoot. Luckily none ever did.

At Tangmere a corner of the aerodrome was given up to them and a cottage as headquarters. Most people at Tangmere thought this was for air-sea rescue.

The plane used was a Westland Lysander with a big extra petrol tank fitted underneath. It was slow but could climb and dive steeply and so could avoid fast fighters and, most important of all, it could land in a small field. It was meant for one passenger but we put in three. Two on the seat - a very tight fit if they were big men - and one at their feet with all the baggage on top of him. The baggage consisted of the Frenchmen's personal cases and sacks of money and vivres - chocolate (imitation French) butter, cigarettes and so on, useful for 'paying' helpers. Sometimes a sack of vivres would be left at Bignor either by mistake or because there were too many other bags. When that happened I always put it in the larder hoping that the Conducting Officer would forget all about it. The chocolate and butter were especially welcome. The baggage was carefully counted and the number chalked up on the side of the plane. This was done because on one of the first ops. a very important packet had been left in the plane and brought back to England.

At the Cottage the men and the baggage were weighed and, if they were even a little over weight, something would have to be left behind. The men's personal belongings were always the first to suffer and many presents or little luxuries they had hoped to take out had to be sacrificed. One artist had to leave his nearly-new box of oil paints behind. This was brought back to Bignor and left in my charge. The artist was arrested and shot and when a local artist, Oliver Hall R.A., had a disastrous fire in his studio, losing many of his pictures and all his materials, I gave the paints to him. I am sure his fellow artist would have approved.

Then the French were given a final briefing and a last drink.

The pilots were nearly all British. At first only men who spoke French were chosen but after a time this had to be given up, although if they did not speak or understand French it could lead to difficulties. Once one of the men going out was a pilot and, in spite of the passenger seat in a Lysander facing backwards, he knew that they were going off course. He tried to tell the pilot over the intercom but he could not make him understand, it was only when he saw the blazing lights of a city that the pilot realized he had gone too far east and was over Geneva. They had used up too much petrol for it to be safe to search for the field and had to fly straight back to Tangmere. Another pilot once lost his way owing to his compass going haywire and he found himself over Manchester.

Not all the pilots who spoke French were very fluent. One of them was showing a Frenchman who had been a pilot, the controls of a Lysander and was overheard to say:

"Vous poussez ça et vous tirez ça et vous mettez ça la et Robert est votre oncle."

But the French were used to being mystified rather then enlightened by English-French.

The most important thing was that the pilot should be good at night navigation as all they had to go on to find the landing field was a description sent over by radio and occasionally, I believe, a photograph taken by the R.A.F. from a considerable altitude. The description of the field was sent over in figures and letters only, based on the clock. This ingenious device was invented by Tony. Each radio operator had a square of perspex marked with lines which enabled him to send over details of the size and shape of the field and the height of trees or buildings around it. With just this description the pilot had to find the field by moonlight and once over the Channel he was on his own with no communication with Tangmere.

When he thought he was over the field be gave a pre-arranged light signal and the 'reception committee', as we called the men who laid on the operation in France, answered if all was well with another pre-arranged signal by flashing a torch and then lit three little hand torches in the shape of an L. That was all the pilot had to land by, touching down at the first torch, taxiing along, turning at the second and stopping at the third torch. If there were six passengers two Lysanders were used, the second landing as soon as the first had taken off. If there were nine passengers they occasionally used three Lysanders but more often a larger plane, a Hudson, but that needed a larger field to land in and was not a popular plane with the pilots. It had to be used even for smaller numbers if they were picking up in the south of France. Once, when the plane had been to Algeria to re-fuel, the pilot brought back some bananas for Tim and Nick, a tremendous treat they could hardly remember having had before.

They got the 'drill' so good that the plane was only on the ground for about a minute and a half. First the baggage was thrown out and counted, then the men got out, the ones coming back got in with their luggage and the all important sacks of courier and they were off. The documents, money and information which passed between France and England were known as 'courier'. Once in their haste, no one remembered to tell them how to shut the sliding 'lid' of the passenger's compartment and they came all the way back, in winter, with it open.

In the meantime the Conducting Officers and the drivers waited at the Cottage, sleeping or talking. The Cottage was staffed by two sergeants, a driver and an old man. The Lysander's 'round trip' took between four and six hours depending on whereabouts in France the field was and how easily the pilot found it. When the Lysander was over the Channel, the pilot was asked if he had had 'joy'. This was done in the form of:

"What colour are you?" If he had been successful he answered "Red"; if he had failed "Blue".

Once a plane was damaged by hitting a tree on take off and the pilot only just managed to bring it home. On being asked his colour he answered, "Pale green".

When they landed they were met by the Conducting Officers and taken to the Cottage with the pilots for a drink. By then it was usually some time between three and four-thirty a.m. Then they rang me up to say they were just starting. If it was Tony he would be sensible and tell me what to expect. He had to be careful as we had no Scrambler on the line to Tangmere.

"We're just coming. A married couple, two men and two unattached females" or whatever it was. All single women were called 'unattached females'. Or if they had failed to find the field he would say:

"No joy, we're coming back."

John, who was the other most frequent Conducting Officer, would never tell me anything. He thought, or pretended to think, that the sex of the new arrivals did not matter to me. He and the rest of the Office thought that the less I knew the better. John and I kept up an affectionate quarrel so that I never knew whether his habit of not telling me things that were important for me to know, was just to annoy me, which it did, or because he really thought it necessary for security.

"We are just coming. Six," he would say and I would have to guess how to arrange the beds.

Back at Bignor, as soon as they had left for Tangmere, I cleared away dinner, washed up and re-laid the table for Reception Pie, as the meal we gave them on arrival came to be called. Then I prepared the meal and tidied the bedrooms if the out-going French had been staying. I did not change the sheets then in case the flight was cancelled and the same lot returned. When all was ready I half undressed and slept on the sofa in the drawing room. At first I used to sleep in my own bed but one morning when the telephone woke me at three-thirty, I fell down our very awkward stairs and after that it seemed safer to sleep downstairs. I hated being woken by the telephone so, if I could, I always set my alarm clock for a little before the time the Lysander was expected back... the Conducting Officer used to tell me when that was. The telephone was such an important and anxious thing that I still panic when it rings and rush to the instrument as though the house were on fire.

As soon as they had rung up I arranged the bedrooms for the new arrivals. My general policy was to give the three big rooms to the French if we were a large party: two in each room if there were six of them or three if there were nine. We had lots of camp beds from the Office, also sheets and horrible army blankets. The drivers slept in the little room - which was once the maid's room - very crowded if there were three of them, and the Conducting Officers and any stray high-ups and I slept in the drawing room on chairs, camp beds, cushions or the sofa. The sofa became known as 'John's bed' and, unless there was a high-up, he always used it and Tony and I slept on camp beds - uncomfortable cold things. And

21

then there was the problem of where the boys should sleep. Very soon after the job began we decided that it would be better if they were weekly boarders at school although, really, they were much too young. Sometimes they had to stay there over a week-end but neither they nor the school liked this and, of course, there were the holidays. In the summer they often slept in a tent in the garden for choice and in the winter a neighbour sometimes put them up, bribing them not to object with a promise of early morning tea in bed, a luxury they never experienced at home. Of course, if there were only three French or even if there were six of convenient sex, the boys slept in their own room.

When the bedrooms were ready and the drawing room tidy, the fires revived and the big coke stove for the water stoked, I finished cooking Reception Pie.

About half-an-hour after ringing up, they would arrive. I always went to the front door to greet them and risked the light showing. It was lovely to welcome old friends who had been through the house before and I prided myself on always remembering them. In the later years of the war men would arrive and greet me by name - Madame Barbara they always called me - and ask after the boys by name. I would think that they had been before and that I had forgotten them and

I would try to pretend I hadn't. Then they would laugh and admit that they had never been before but had been told all about the set-up at Bignor, while waiting in France for the Lysander.

The number of presents they brought us was embarrassing. Innumerable books and bottles of wine and brandy for Tony, all marked "Pour la Victoire" and all sorts of lovely things for me: scent, nylons, brooches, chocolates, flowers. Perhaps the present I valued most was the bunch of lily-of-the-valley I found on my plate at breakfast one May Day. They had been picked in France the night before, following the charming French habit of giving Our Lady's Tears on the first of her month. It was amazing that these people who were often 'on the run' and always in constant danger of arrest, found time to choose presents for us and burden themselves with extra things in the small case that was all they could bring with them. They also brought us two little wooden models, one of a Lysander and one of a Hudson that had been made by referring to postcard reproductions.

On one occasion a new arrival came into the drawing room and drew back the curtains saying:

"How wonderful to be in free England."

As the light went streaming out the Air Raid Warden came rushing up. If he reported us to the police nothing happened; we were told after the war that the police had been told not to take any notice of strange goings on at Bignor Manor.

I was always disappointed if no 'bods', as we called the French, arrived but only sacks of courier though I knew they were of the greatest importance. Once, early in 1944, only several large knobbly sacks arrived. These were rushed up to London after an early breakfast. Much later I was told that they contained all the bits of a V.1., an unmanned flying bomb, popularly known as a 'doodlebug', if *popular* is the word I want.

When the 'bod' had been given a drink we had Reception Pie. Often men who had never been to the house before would ask on arrival "What have we got for Reception Pie?" By the time this was over it was generally about five or five-thirty and if possible we hurried them off to bed. This was not always easy in the summer when it was already light but we generally managed to remind them how tired they were. Having settled the French and their drivers upstairs, the rest of us flopped into 'bed' in the drawing room.

Breakfast would usually be late unless someone had to get to London early. I always enjoyed it when they came down in the morning and found their way to the kitchen, attracted by the smell of bacon and real coffee. Often they had been hiding in farm buildings for several days and nights waiting for the op. to be 'on', so they were wonderfully appreciative of the comparative comfort of Bignor and even accepted being three in a room. After the terrible shortages of food in France they revelled in such simple things as we were able to give them; especially in real coffee after the barley or acorn coffee to which they were accustomed. This meal spread over a long time if there were a lot of them and they came down at different times. Then the 'huddles' started. The Conducting Officers or the French high-ups who came down to meet rather important French in-comers, always liked to have preliminary talks with the agents in the comparative peace and quiet of Bignor. These talks were called 'huddles'. This meant that the drawing room had to be tidied while breakfast was going on in winter but in the summer they 'huddled' in the garden. One of Tony's jobs was to collect small change, Metro tickets and things of that sort from the in-comers to give to the next lot of out-goers.

After breakfast those not 'huddling' cleaned their shoes outside the front door. These were often very muddy from the landing field in France. I collected this mud and grew mustard and cress on it so that I could offer salad grown on French soil to the next moon's French.

If we were lucky they would go up to London before lunch which was a great relief if a new party was expected that afternoon. In the summer there were perhaps three or four ops. in a moon period but in the winter only one or two, if that.

While they were 'huddling' I would be very good and patient and wait until about eleven-thirty before asking if they would want lunch.

"We're still talking. I don't know," the Officer would say.

I would wait till mid-day and then try again, with the same unsatisfactory result. At five minutes to one they would come in and say:

"Yes, please, lunch now."

So I generally prepared something just in case.

If people arrived who had not been expected, they generally had to stay at Bignor while someone rushed up to London to make identity cards for them. Once a man arrived who was suspected of being a double-agent and Tony had to stay down and question him. That was very uncomfortable. Of course I was never told the result of the questioning.

2

That is how an operation went if all went well but lots of things could go wrong and they often did. The most frequent trouble was the weather. Those at Tangmere would ring up after the two-thirty or seven-thirty weather forecast, better known as the 'Met. Report', and say, "C'est off. It's going to be a fog." When the group arrived from London I would have to greet them with this disappointing news or, if it was the later time, it would be in the middle of dinner, when they were all packed up and ready to go. Then we would have a jolly evening. Some would play darts; perhaps four would play bridge; two would dance; generally one would sit and read poetry; the radio would blare and everyone would talk ceaselessly. Or we would all play progressive ping-pong in the dining room. The ping-pong table-top was often already on the dining table to make it big enough.

Sometimes the bad weather would go on for days or even for the whole two weeks of a moon period. The French would have to be kept occupied. They were naturally rather strung up and apt to get on each other's nerves. Darts were a great stand-by. The French took to the game in a big way and most days a party would go to the White Horse in Sutton and play, not getting back to lunch until after closing time, which was a bore as there were often one or two who didn't go and, becoming hungry, had to be fed separately.

When operations were off, the pilots also needed their morale kept up so we often had Pilots' Parties. Generally, about four or five of them would come over from Tangmere and then there was real pandemonium. Darts, bridge, dancing and ping-pong with someone reading and the infernal radio at full blast. They always brought beer and cigarettes with them. After dinner they washed up for me. One washed, two dried and the rest stood at strategic points between the sink and the cupboard in the dining room where the plates were kept. The plates were thrown from one to the other. Nothing was ever broken but I was always terrified as we had no spare crockery, in fact not nearly enough.

The pilots' driver, Elston, brought them and returned for them again at about midnight. Then we ended by singing all the well-known French songs that are easy, even for those who know no French - Allouette, Les Chevaliers de la Table Ronde, Sur le pont....

If a group was with us over a Sunday one or two would ask to be taken to Mass at Petworth or Arundel.

A less generally popular occupation than the pub, was a walk on the Downs. Tony and Duff-the-dog always favoured this and so did I if I had time. If things became very desperate we would go to Chichester or Brighton. Some people remained perfectly calm, and were content to sit and read all day. Luckily we had a great many French books in the house and after someone noticed that we had nothing for the lovers of crime, a man brought us over six books by Simenon. A few men liked gardening, a thing I always encouraged enthusiastically. I don't know how I should have managed without this occasional help.

Sometimes Tony took one or two riding. They hired horses from a small local stables. Once he went with a French Cavalry Officer and André, a Jockey. Tony had his stirrups at the usual English height, the Cavalry Officer put them at full length and the jockey put them right up and sat on the horse's neck. He chose the least good horse but before they had crossed the first field he was out of sight and they didn't see him again until they returned to the stables. He drew more speed out of that horse than anyone knew it had in it.

A worse thing than the weather breaking and causing an op. to be cancelled was when the Office rang up in the middle of dinner to say that someone had been arrested. They could not know if he had talked under torture and had made it unsafe for them to go. Those were terrible evenings - far from jolly. The French did not know if their friends or relations had been given away and longed to be out there with them.

All the way through the job the knowledge that those arrested would be tortured, was a horrible thought at the back of our minds; seldom mentioned but always present. I was told afterwards that, on the whole, it was the highly intelligent, sensitive ones that withstood torture best, not the 'tough guys'. One man told us that he tried to visualize where the spots on our Dalmatian were, to take his mind off what they were doing to him. Some who had been tortured more than once said that it was the smaller things that were hardest to bear; such as pulling out teeth or nails or sticking pins into a woman's breast - not the beatings, hanging by the wrists, electric shocks or near-drownings. These made them semi-unconscious after a time. Most agreed that if you could withstand the first quarter-of-an-hour without talking you probably wouldn't talk at all. The very worst moment must have been when they fetched a man for a second session and he knew what to expect.

It was this threat of torture hanging over them that made their cheerful courage so moving. The bravest of all were the Jews who were in danger of being arrested just because they were Jews, as well as for their resistance work. One, whom we knew very well, another André, missed a moon owing to bad weather. He was parachuted out, without any previous training, in the dark period and made his first jump into Occupied France.

Another problem that fairly often arose was the failure to find the landing field or to find the Reception Committee signalling that it was not safe to land. When that happened the French who had gone out so courageously and hopefully would come back very tired and depressed and have to try again the next night, or sometimes go back to London and wait for the next moon.

Some people tried as many as three times and had to return. On one of these occasions the first op. was cancelled when they were already at Tangmere, the second time they failed to find the field and the third time they landed successfully but found they were behind our advancing forces. There was one poor girl who was not top priority and came down to Bignor twice expecting to go out and both times someone else was put in her place at the last minute.

Then, of course, there were accidents. The most frequent and least serious was the aircraft getting bogged down in a wet field in France. It is comparatively easy to estimate the size of a field accurately and the height of trees or buildings but much more difficult to estimate the firmness of the ground. On one occasion when a plane was stuck they fetched oxen to try and tow it to firmer ground and when they failed, two more oxen were added; even that was not enough and finally the pilot had to puncture the extra petrol tank and set fire to the plane. This pilot was Robin. During the weeks till an op. could be laid on to bring him back he hid at a farm, only venturing out after dark until he got desperate for books and, evading his kind host, went to the nearest town and bought some. All the pilots who got bogged down returned safely.

A very blond Scandinavian pilot once had to make a forced landing in France. He did not speak a word of French so when he and his 'passengers' had to go by train to a safer district, they pretended that he was deaf and dumb. He

Bignor Manor

The White Horse, Sutton

The Sitting Room
with dartboard and
secret cupboard

Anthony, Barbara and
Timothy Bertram

The Sitting Room

Timothy with one
of the French Agents
known as Duke and
Duff-the-dog

The Dining Room

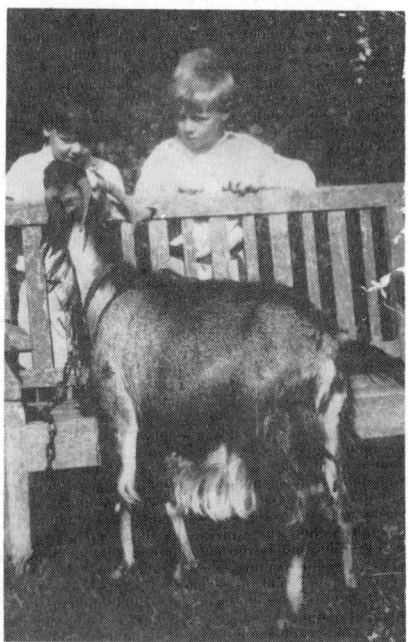

Timothy and Nicholas
with Caroline-the-goat

spent the whole day holding up a newspaper without being able to read a word of it.

There were many very much more serious accidents. One Lysander was shot down into the sea and the pilot and one passenger drowned; also, after D-Day, one was shot down in France by our own side. One serious accident was on the landing field. It was a double op., six French went out in two Lysanders. At dinner that night I asked the man sitting next to me to bring some French stamps the next time he came over as Tim had just started to collect. They went off with their usual courage. The first plane to land overshot the mark into a ploughed field, turned over and burst into flames. The pilot was killed outright, two of the three passengers were thrown clear unhurt; the reception party could not approach the burning plane so they collected the two unhurt men and went off as quickly as possible before the Germans were attracted by the blaze. The second plane returned without attempting to land. The third passenger, Lestanges, somehow managed to fight his way out of the burning plane and found himself alone in a ploughed field in a part of France he did not know and badly burnt up both arms. He did what they had been told to do in emergencies, he went to the village priest. The priest took him in, saw that he was badly burnt and needed urgent medical attention. However, he knew that the local doctor was a sympathiser with the Germans. So he put Lestanges on a bicycle and pushed him four or five miles to a little Convent Nursing Home. There, the Mother Superior took him in, put him in a locked room and attended to him herself, not allowing any one else in. To account for this secrecy, she herself started the rumour that it was one of her nuns having a baby. The priest got in touch with Lestanges' friends in Paris who got in touch with London and we laid on an op. to bring him home three weeks after his accident. He spent those three weeks desperately ill with his burns. We had an ambulance waiting at Tangmere to take him to East Grinstead hospital. As he got in he handed the Conducting Officer an envelope to be given to me. In it were the stamps I had asked for. Of course, I went to see him at East Grinstead and when I thanked him for the stamps I found he did not remember anything about them at all. I could not, of course, give them to the boys until after the war. I am glad that, after the war, Lestanges returned to the village where the Convent Nursing Home was and told people what had really happened in the locked room.

The worst night was when Stephen was killed. Stephen was the son of very old friends of my family and I had known him since he was a baby.

The night he was killed, three Lysanders went out with nine French who all came down to Bignor first. One car-load was late because neither the Conducting Officer nor the driver knew the way. It was not one of our regular girl drivers but a strange man. I fed and saw off the two car-loads that arrived punctually and then cut sandwiches for the late ones so that they could go on to Tangmere the moment they arrived. When at last they turned up the Conducting Officer asked me to go with them to show them the way. When we approached the guard at the entrance to the aerodrome I was told to crouch down at the back under the legs of the French, as they had no pass for me. This was the only time I saw off a Lysander. We arrived only just in time, after the others had been given their last drink and final instructions and were walking out to the aircraft.

When they had taken off - three great dragonflies of the night - I was taken to the Cottage for a drink and then driven back to Bignor to prepare Reception Pie. One French girl, Little Ben, had not gone out at the last moment and was still there.

The night passed as usual and my clock woke me at the time I had been told they should get in. I waited for the telephone call getting more and more anxious as it got later and later. At last, at about seven, Tony rang. I could tell at once by his voice that something awful had happened.

"I'm coming with two," he said.

That was all. *Two* from a triple op. and why, "*I'm* coming," when there were three Officers and three drivers? When he arrived he said, "They're very tired," and we had Reception Pie in silence instead of the usual excited hubbub. At last they went to bed and I was able to ask the question that had been hammering at my head:

"What's happened?"

"Stephen's been killed and MacBride and Berthaud and Cazenave. I'll tell you later," and he flopped into bed exhausted.

What had happened was that, for once, the Met. report was wrong and before the planes returned a fog had come down. A hundred British planes crashed that night. One of ours containing only one passenger, the pilot Robin who had been bogged down in France the moon before, arrived early before the fog. The other two were returning successfully, each with two passengers. Unfortunately, when they reached Tangmere the fog was very low and thick. One crashed near the aerodrome killing the pilot, MacBride, but not the two passengers; the other Lysander was diverted to Ford airfield nearby where it crashed killing the pilot, Stephen, and both passengers. Tony and John Hunt, the local

Security Officer, had to find the crashed plane and identify the charred bodies.

Later in the morning Robin, one Conducting Officer and a driver came to Bignor on their way to London bringing the blood stained and partially burnt sacks of courier. The other car went straight to London from Tangmere.

Little Ben was not told of the accident as she was to go out on the next op. and they did not want to make her nervous. Of course she must have guessed from the atmosphere that something had happened.

I could not go to Stephen's funeral as I had to take Nicky to a doctor in London that day. I met Little Ben for lunch and still had to pretend I did not know what had happened. I took Elizabeth, Stephen's wife, to the interment of the two Frenchmen. It was a wartime affair with two other men buried with them. The brief ceremony was conducted by both a Catholic and an Anglican priest, and a Rabbi. The Last Post was sounded and a volley fired.

3

One of the things that made the job so very interesting from our point of view was that we had every kind of Frenchman and woman through the house. I don't think there was any age, profession, occupation or district of France that was not represented. We had a priest and a seminarian, doctors, nurses, artists, writers and journalists; school masters and mistresses, dressmakers, a perfume manufacturer and a Champagne grower, housewives, peasants, diplomats, Members of Parliament, lawyers, policemen; motor mechanics and garage owners, soldiers, sailors and airmen, a duke, a princess and a brothel keeper. We had people from every corner of France with every variety of dialect and of course people of every political opinion from Communist to Royalist.

This sometimes led to difficulties if the op. was off for several nights running, which often happened. Once we had in the house an elderly, aristocratic and very conservative Colonel, a Communist journalist and a young motor mechanic. I was really sorry for the motor mechanic. His only interest was racing cars and as he did not have one he just sat doing absolutely nothing for two weeks. He didn't even read and was one of the few French who didn't take to darts. The Colonel went for a walk to the right and the Communist to the left and they glared at each other at meals. But on the third or fourth day they came back from their walks beaming from ear to ear. The Colonel came to us and said, "Do you know, that Communist is a nice man," and the Communist came to us and said, "Do you know, the Colonel's intelligent." After that things went better.

Another time when we had six delayed for several days, the tension became so great that Tony had to take a party to Brighton and I had to take the rest to Chichester to prevent bloodshed. It was not surprising that they were on edge. One man nearly drove us mad by walking up and down the room ceaselessly. I think it was he who had a purse made out of a German's skin. There was an awful moment when I thought he was going to give it to me.

One October we had three men in the house for the whole moon period. We had lovely sunny days and thick fog every night so that every day they were hopeful and every night disappointed. One of them, Brutus, said he would be perfectly happy if he could shoot. So we borrowed a gun and cartridges and asked Lord Mersey, our neighbour at Bignor Park, if he could shoot rabbits on his estate. Lord Mersey agreed provided it was only rabbits. The first few days Brutus brought in three or four rabbits and then one day he produced a pheasant from under his coat which, he said, had flown between him and a rabbit. Lovely. On the last day of the moon when they either would have to go or return to London he asked me what I would really like if he had been allowed to shoot anything. Knowing what there was likely to be I said "Wild duck." Sure enough four ducks flew between him and a rabbit.

One night as a middle-aged man was helped out of the Lysander he said, "Ripping, spiffing, tophole." He had been at an English prep-school and never forgotten it. Every morning after his cold bath he did dumbbell exercises. He stayed several days at Bignor and insisted on going to Chichester to buy boxing gloves for the boys - the first and last time they ever put them on. He was well-known as an Anglophile in his part of

France so there was no point in trying to change him. He asked for a bull dog to be parachuted out to him - he did not get it. Later he had to 'disappear' so he grew a grey beard but still bicycled energetically everywhere, unfortunately he forgot to disguise his comparatively young hands and was arrested.

One man who came several times and who we got to know well afterwards, was an enormous farmer called Arlières. Driven out of his farm in the north of France by the Germans he went further south and bought another farm. On arriving at Bignor, after Reception Pie, he refused to go to bed and walked off round the farm and met the farmer, also a big man. We never knew how they communicated with each other but Arlières came back with information about the farm and great scorn for English farm buildings. He was enormous and looked clumsy. He broke the seat of a Lysander during training but he could be quick and agile. When he went out again he was arrested and told to get into a lorry. Pretending to be as stiff and awkward as he looked, he was helped in by the Germans. They were right out in the country when he suddenly leapt out of the lorry and ran. Instead of hiding in a wood he ran through it into a field of maize and lay down scattering pepper - "Which, naturally, I had with me" - in case they brought dogs. The Germans searched the wood and then gave up. Arlières went to another part of France and bought another farm.

One of my happiest memories is of Pierre-le-paysan. He was a radio operator. When he had completed his training he was not quite quick enough to be sent out, so he came down to Bignor to practice. He installed his transmitting set in the attic and practised daily. When he had finished he asked me if, please, he might do a little work in my garden. I did not insult him by telling him what needed to be done, I just showed him the tool shed. I have never had my garden so beautifully cared for. When he could do no more, he scythed all the long grass he could find and stacked it for Caroline-the-goat and also stinging nettles for both Caroline and the chickens. Then he asked if perhaps I had a friend he could help. I sent him to our friends the Armstrongs in Sutton, where he worked in their garden and scythed their long grass. He borrowed a dust sheet from Jesse Armstrong, bundled the grass up in it and carried it on his back up to Bignor. Between Sutton and Bignor there is a hill of one in six. Nothing daunted, he returned for a second load. In this way he was perfectly happy all day but in the evening he didn't know what to do with himself. He would sit playing out the wool for me as I knitted and would tell me how to make eau de vie and how to bottle peas. I wonder why we thought that home-bottled peas are bound to be poisonous while the French ate them freely. He soon became a first-class transmitter and was sent out to France. He was very conscientious and continued transmitting although he knew a detecting car was circling nearer and nearer. He was shot while still trying to get his message finished. As he was known as a Resistance worker it was safe only for his family to attend his funeral but in every window along the route to the cemetery there was a bunch of flowers.

While at Bignor he received, through the Red Cross I think, a letter from his wife addressed to her sister in Switzerland but really meant for him. It was a wonderful letter full of all the family news he longed to hear and full of her love. She only mentioned him to say that he was away but one could tell it was all meant for him. He was so pleased with it and so proud of his wife.

He left for France rather suddenly after his stay with us. There was no time for him to go to a town to buy me a present so he asked me if I would accept ten shillings to buy myself one. I did.

Another very special friend was André-le-Jockey. He was half-English and had been a private in the Durham Light Infantry with

Tony. When Tony was moved to the War Office he remembered this totally bilingual man and recruited him for our work. He spoke perfect French and perfect Cockney. He had been a jockey at Chantilly. Before he went for parachute training the doctor who examined him to see if he was fit enough to jump asked if he had ever broken a limb. "Two arms, a collar bone and a leg," said André cheerfully. He became an extremely successful Resistance worker and ended as an Officer decorated by both French and British. After a very good dinner he and Tony had together in Paris in 1945, he asked Tony if he would like to ride a race horse the next day. Of course Tony enthusiastically said he would but in the cold reality of the next morning he rang up André to ask if he really meant it. "No, sir," said André. It was he who sent me the lily-of-the-valley.

Once an elderly Member of Parliament arrived with his mistress although he had been told she was not to come. At breakfast she dunked his bread in his coffee and fed him with it.

Also there was a man who arrived with jaundice and had to stay down at Bignor, in bed, for several days. We sent for a strange doctor, not the one we had. I suppose we thought it better for security reasons, I wonder why?

Another man who came several times was Gilbert Renault-Roulier, who was known as Rémy. His first trip over was made by boat and later he brought his wife and several small children over by boat too but he frequently made the trip by Lysander. He arrived once with a pot-plant for Madame de Gaulle who lived in England during part of the War. The first time he arrived in London he went to the French church off Leicester Square which had been destroyed by a bomb. He found the statue of Our Lady broken but the head was intact. The next time he went back by Lysander he took the head with him although it was very heavy and the strict weight limit must have meant he could take very little else. He took it to a sculptor friend who made a body to fit it - the first thing imported from France after the war was the complete statue with the old head and a new body.

The last time he went out it was thought necessary that he should be disguised. His réseau had been betrayed and nearly all the members of the cell arrested, it was very dangerous for him to go at all. After his appearance had been altered he walked past his wife and children in the Park, who knew nothing of his plans, and they did not recognize him, so his disguise was considered good enough. Then he came down to Bignor and as he walked up the path I recognized him at once and greeted him by name.   The Conducting Officer looked horrified and hurriedly took me aside and asked if I had been told he was coming. When I said "No", we agreed that I had better pretend to Rémy that I had been told so as not to spoil his confidence in his disguise.   I was told later that he had refused to have his teeth out to alter his mouth and I think that I always look at a man's mouth more than any other feature as I am partially deaf and lip read.

Popeye and Pierre Brossolette were among the first men to pass through Bignor. Popeye was Jacques Robert. He and Pierre Brossolette known as 'Pierre-le-gris', came unexpectedly and I had to keep them at Bignor while someone went to London to make them identity cards. I was told not to let them out of the garden. The second day a bomb fell near Portsmouth and cut out the electricity. As we cooked by this means I was at my wits end. I managed a cold lunch but by the evening they were loudly demanding a hot dinner. In fear and trembling I took them down to a little guest house in the village which I knew had an Aga.   It was full of self-evacuated old ladies. Popeye and Pierre-le-gris chose to believe that none of them would understand French and made the most awful remarks about them and told most unsuitable stories.   I sat in embarrassed fury knowing that it would make them worse if I tried to stop them. Luckily, the next morning, I was told to take them to London - without stopping on the way. I resisted them through the first four or five villages and then one of them pretended to have an urgent call of nature and at the next pub we stopped. I never dared confess this to the Office. After that all went well until, in the outskirts of London, I exceeded the speed limit and was stopped by the Police. As neither of the Frenchmen spoke English I was terrified that the policeman would ask them something, also I could feel Popeye longing to get out and fight the poor man. I think even he realized he must be careful and it passed off alright.

The name Popeye stuck to him after he had received parachute training. Being a big man, Jacques was given an extra large parachute and he came down very slowly shouting out, "I'm Popeye the sailor man."

Brossolette went out again and was arrested. He was tortured and didn't talk but when they came to fetch him for a second session, he felt unable to face it again and threw himself over the bannister of a high staircase. There is a street named after him in Paris.

And there was the beautiful Marie Madeleine. She came several times and never looked the same twice running - sometimes red-haired and sometimes black, but always elegant and lovely.

On one occasion she went over to France but the pilot failed to find the field and they had to return. In the car from Tangmere to Bignor at four in the morning she was sitting between Tony and another Conducting Officer:

"One of you was educated by the Benedictines and one by the Jesuits," she said, "Which was which?"

"I was at a Benedictine school," said Tony.

"Then I shall sleep on your shoulder," she said and promptly did so.

One day she came down to Bignor, not to go out herself but to meet someone coming in. We sat up all night talking and she told me of all the horrors of torture. She became the head of one of the biggest réseaux. Her book, "Noah's Ark" is one of the very best of the many books written about this terrible but fascinating war.

A man who came several times was a high-ranking police officer who managed to release several Resistance workers from prison. When he was coming over here he used to tell his Office that he was going to the Riviera for a week or two's rest, so it was vital for him to get back during the same moon if he was not to over-stay his leave.

Another man wished it to be thought that he was in England when he had really returned to

France - so he recorded a speech which the B.B.C. put out after he had left.

One man told me that before coming over he had sold his house to a collaborator so that, after the war, he could shoot the man and have his house back!

And there were the Marx Brothers. Three French policemen arrived one night dressed in all sorts of odd clothes. They had let some of our men out of prison so it wasn't safe for them to stay in France. They had arrived at the last minute as a substitute for three other men in less danger.

Another time, two men turned up in the middle of the summer in skiing clothes. They were policemen, too, and no other civilian clothes could be found for them in a hurry.

Once a man arrived who didn't want his true identity known in England. In the morning I saw a metal disk in the lavatory pan so, of course, I fished it out and gave it to the Conducting Officer, unintentionally giving away the poor man's secret. I hope it did not really harm him, of course I was not told.

As well as every kind of French man or woman, we had every kind of worker in the Resistance movement. The Resistance was organized in watertight networks - réseaux - so that the members of one network didn't know the members of another. Thus, if they talked under torture, they could only give away a limited number of people. Sometimes two members of one family were in different networks, neither knowing that the other was in the Resistance. We usually had only members of one réseau at a time at Bignor but once or twice we had men from two different ones. When this happened, they arrived at different times and the first group were fed and in bed before the second group came and, in the morning, the first ones had an early breakfast and went off to London before the others were up. This arrangement was carefully explained to them and was, of course, entirely for their own safety; but on one occasion I went into the bathroom to fetch something before the first breakfast and found all six of them in there together. Breakfast was eaten in stony silence, the men all looking like naughty schoolboys.

The head of the groups were the ones we grew to know best as they went backwards and forwards frequently. Some of them were allowed to bring their wives and children over. The poor children used to arrive very tired, bewildered and frightened because it was not possible to explain to them beforehand what was going to happen. Two small boys once arrived in a dreadful state. They had both been air sick and they were both terrified. Without being told anything they had been taken to a farm and hidden for two days in a hay barn. In the middle of the night they were woken, taken to a field and bundled into a plane at their parents' feet with luggage on top of them. When they got to Tangmere they heard everyone speaking a strange language and the poor little boys thought they had been taken to Germany. In the excitement of arrival at Tangmere their parents had forgotten to tell them what had happened.

On the other hand Popeye's two girls arrived bright and gay and spick and span. The elder one, about eight I think, began speaking English at once. They were thrilled to be lent real boys' pyjamas to sleep in. For some unknown reason the operator in France had told them that the Holy Ghost was coming for them. A few days after they were settled in London, the girls were discovered in Hyde Park playing 'Holy Ghosts' with outstretched arms and engine-like noises in the way all children indicate aeroplanes. This was thought so dangerous for security reasons that they were hurriedly taken to the country.

The largest number of Resistance workers were, I suppose, the men who were to find out information of use to the allies - the object of the whole concern, of course. These went somewhere when they left us, to be told what to look for and how to look for it.

Then there were the radio operators. They were a vital and very dangerous link; the information collected had to be transmitted to Britain, with instructions about operations, from the French end. They had, I believe, a quarter-of-an-hour a day during which they could get in touch with London on a special wave-length and if they missed that they had to wait until the next day. As the information was often of extreme urgency they did their utmost to get it out. The casualties among this group were very high. They were often shot while still trying to get their message finished.

The people who laid on the operations in France - the Reception Committee - were my husband's concern in the dark periods. They went up to a place in Huntingdonshire and all day practised estimating the size of fields (they could not pace them as that might be seen and would look very conspicuous except, some insisted, in the mushroom season) and the height of trees and buildings and, as well as they could, the firmness of the ground. The Reception Committee was in complete control during an op. and a General told us once how splendid it was that one of them, whom he knew to be a private soldier, had ordered him, a General, to put out the cigarette he had lit on the field.

At dusk, to get as near moonlight as possible without a moon, the pilots practised landing with just three little hand torches while the French were drilled in getting in and out of Lysanders quickly and in not forgetting to count each item of baggage as it was thrown out. It was an exhausting time in the summer, as they rarely got to bed before one or two because, with double summer-time, it was dusk until nearly midnight.

In theory I was free in the dark period but it didn't always work like that. There were people who had been ill or who were tired and needed the rest and quiet of Bignor before going out again and there were radio operators who had finished their training but were not quite quick enough, so they were sent down to me to practise, like Pierre-le-paysan.

But, of course, I was sometimes free and once or twice went away for a rest. A particularly lovely holiday was one September when we all went to the Scilly Isles. Visitors were not allowed there during the war, so we were the only ones on St. Martin's for a glorious two weeks of beautiful weather. Tony had been there the winter before and was brought back by a Lysander. The pilot said he would bring him right on to Bignor as there was sure to be a field big enough to land on.

There is a very big field but the farmer had put up posts to prevent enemy landings: the Lysander landed between the posts.

4

At the time I was told nothing. I did not know people's names, where they came from, where they were going to or, above all, what they were doing. It was only afterwards that I was told a little.

A great many of our people were arrested and tortured. A lot were shot, a lot sent to prisons or concentration camps but a lot escaped by some quick-wittedness.

One radio operator was travelling by train with his transmitting set in a small suitcase on the rack. The Germans came through the train, opening cases. They pointed to his case and asked what was in it. He looked them straight in the face and said:

"It's a transmitting set for sending secret messages to England." The French in the carriage laughed, the Germans laughed too and went out.

One man was arrested in Paris on a very wet day when his hat and mackintosh were soaking wet. He knew that he had in his pocket a paper that incriminated not only himself but several of his friends. He was taken straight to the Gestapo headquarters for questioning. As he went in he saw a row of pegs so he took off his wet hat and coat and hung them up. Then he was searched and when they found nothing they said they were sorry, they had arrested the wrong man, he could go. He bowed very politely, picked up his hat and coat on the way out and left. The paper was still in his mackintosh pocket.

The network of sympathisers enabled news to be passed out of prisons and hospitals with great speed and accuracy. One man was wounded when he was arrested and was taken to hospital before being taken for questioning. After a day or so, his friends heard that he was to be collected by the Gestapo at ten o'clock the next morning. At three minutes to ten they turned up in a stolen Gestapo car and stolen uniforms. They asked for Monsieur 'So-and-so', who was handed over to them, and they drove out of one gate as the real Gestapo drove in at the other.

A girl who lived in central France had the rather dull job of taking a suitcase, of whose contents she knew nothing, to Paris. It was given to her by a man she didn't know and she had to take it to an address in Paris and deliver it to another man she didn't know. The case contained papers - the information collected by many agents and was heavy, so she used to borrow her sister's one-year-old baby. When she got to the control at the station in Paris, which was the danger point and where she had to show her papers, she would look round for a nice-looking young German soldier and smiling sweetly - she was a very pretty girl - she would ask him to carry her heavy case through for her as, with the baby, she couldn't get at her papers. He would take it through without question and she would thank him with another smile and then disappear into the crowd.

One day when an operator went to see that all was well with the landing ground for that night, he found workmen building a wall across the field. The Germans had realised that it was large enough for planes to land on. The men were persuaded to work as slowly as possible and when night fell the operators joined the workmen in removing what they had built. After the successful rendezvous they built it up again. Another time a farmer was ordered to build a haystack in the centre of a field. Knowing that the field was used for Lysander landings, the farmer built the stack on a platform with wheels so that it could easily be removed for an op. and put back again afterwards.

I think Germans appeared on the landing field only once. As the plane was approaching, each operator found an armed German behind him. They were ordered to give the correct signal for 'all clear' for landing. They gave a wrong signal but the pilot was sure it was the right field and, as the Reception Committee were forced to light the three torches, it looked alright so he came in to land. Before he had stopped one of the Germans fired at him and missed so he opened up the throttle again and took off, pursued by the Germans all firing their revolvers at him. In the confusion the French escaped. The plane was damaged but with great skill the pilot brought it home. I think that was the time he had to swoop up and down all the way back. Another pilot who had spent too much time looking for the field, landed in the west of England, not at Tangmere, with the last drop of petrol in his tank.

5

One of my great problems was food. We had a big vegetable and fruit garden and we kept chickens, rabbits, bees and a goat, which helped, and the Office occasionally sent down whisky, gin, tins of butter and horrible Grade-3 salmon. When the job started they made me a Catering Establishment like an hotel. That meant I had to fill in innumerable forms every month with the number of main meals, subsidiary meals, drinks, beverages and I don't know what. They explained to me that as all my 'visitors' were in the Forces they were entitled to a higher ration than the civilian one, so they told me that if I could not get enough food I could cheat on my Food Office returns but I was not to let the Food Office know I was cheating. One got rations one month for what one had eaten the month before, so it worked out in the end - but not at the time. My returns were like a fever chart. When the boys were at school and in the dark period it would be one, one, one for every meal, and then suddenly, at the beginning of a moon period, twelve or thirteen for three main meals a day. Very cautiously I would add a few here and a few there and get a little extra but I was terrified of the Food Office who sent someone every month to sign the books. I would sit biting my nails, hoping they would not ask awkward questions while they went through the forms. After the war I went to the local Food Office and asked the head woman if she had found my forms very muddled and confused. "Oh no," she said, "I was told never to look at them. I only signed them." If only I had known... Even so, I sometimes had to kill a laying hen. I usually shopped in Petworth for anything the village shop could not supply and when we had big parties down I often went to Chichester, where one was more likely to find something 'off the ration'. Once coming back from a fruitless visit there I met a keeper with rabbits hanging from a stick over his shoulder and bought the lot.

On these expeditions to Chichester I always hoped to meet John Hunt, the pianist. As he was Security Officer for the district he was 'in the Secret' and often came over to Bignor. These visits were nicest in the dark period, then we could go down to our friends in Sutton, Martin and Jesse Armstrong, and he would play to us on their piano. He sometimes gave recitals in Chichester Cathedral which were lovely interludes in war time life.

Caroline-the-goat was a continual worry, she was always having to be milked, or fed or tied up, or worse still, taken to the Billy. It is almost impossible to tie up a goat if there are roses or apple trees in sight but her favourite food was peach trees. She became a well-known character. Often the pilots would come over in their Lysanders if an op. was cancelled and swoop down much too low over Bignor, even once or twice flying under the telephone wires. This always alarmed Caroline - but not so much as it did me - so when she was expecting a kid, an order was put up in the Flight's headquarters at Tangmere forbidding any low-flying over Bignor until Caroline was safely delivered.

She achieved greater fame later when an operation was named after her. The B.B.C. broadcast Les Messages Personnels every night - a programme used by the Office to send coded messages to Resistance workers giving information about our ops. In case of 'Operation Caroline' the news that the operation was 'on' was conveyed by the use of the word 'blue' in connection with 'Caroline'. For nights the message said:

"Caroline has a new hat."

"Caroline is well."

"Caroline went for a walk."

and finally, "Caroline has a blue dress."

When we were in Paris after the war many French Resistance workers who had never been through the house would ask how Caroline was.

Another of my worries was the question of help. Sometimes girls from the village came to wash up but in such a small village there were not many of the right age. As soon as they left school they joined the NAAFI or something similar and the ones that did come were never very reliable. Early in 1944, the Office at last realized that feeding such big numbers and doing all the housework was a bit too much for me. They built an enormous double Nissen hut in the orchard so that we could have room for residential help. It was at least twice as big as we could possible want. Another stupidity was to tell the Office of Works' men who came to put it up that it was for the fire fighters. A double Nissen hut for fire fighters in a village of 130 inhabitants! Of course Tim and Nick went out to help them put it up and of course they told the men that it was for the French. The Office really could not have blamed us if that had caused a security leak. When it was ready Tony and I thought we would sleep there instead of in the drawing room - they had supplied camp beds. We soon found that one cannot sleep in an unheated Nissen hut in January and we went back to the stuffy but warm house. However, the problem of help did now seem soluble, when they had remembered the heaters.

The first person they sent down was a delightful, very smart, fully-trained, high-grade secretary who had never washed-up in her life and had been told she was to help entertain the French - although she did help that evening, she went back the next day. Then they sent two French women in the dark period. I fetched them from the station on a Sunday night having left supper all ready on the table. They seemed pleasant. When we went to bed they asked me what time we had breakfast.

"Seven-thirty, tomorrow," I said, "The boys have to be got off to school."

At seven-thirty there was no sign of them, so we had breakfast and I took the boys to school. At about nine-thirty they appeared and looked at the cleared dining room table and said, "Where's breakfast?" I pointed to the kitchen and went into the garden. I gave them ample time for breakfast and then went in and said brightly, "Now, the first thing I want you to do is to scrub the brick floors in the dining room and hall." They looked at me in horror. "We don't do that sort of work," they said, "We've come to help entertain the French." They went back that day.

Then they sent me a French soldier, Jean Théoclist. He was perfection, he played with the boys, cooked, did the housework, did the garden and he was a delightful person. He had just come out of hospital after a head wound and when he had given me four days of bliss, he hit his head on a beam and had to go back to hospital. After that they decided I was not meant to have help.

Luckily I was very rarely ill all through those years. Once, as I changed just before the arrival of a big party, I discovered I was covered with spots. Having had measles, I supposed it was German measles. I put on a high-necked jersey and hoped for the best. I didn't feel ill but when I went to put food in the oven I found I was unable to bend my knees, they had blown up like footballs. There was the time I had a tooth out and nearly took an overdose of pain killers because my jaw went septic and I was trying to be ready for a moon. The only other time I remember being ill was worse. I had a miscarriage in the middle of a busy moon. That time I did feel ill.

One minor difficulty was our shortage of crockery and cutlery. The Office sent us sheets, blankets and camp beds but refused to send other household crockery. This often meant having to wash up between courses and we always had to use cracked plates and cups without handles. We could not, of course, buy crockery at that stage of the war. When our job was over the Office sent a crate of miscellaneous things - 47 saucers, 21 cups, 19 plates and 8 milk jugs, all hideous canteen china.

The question of security was another difficulty. Our 'cover' was that I ran a Convalescent home for French Officers and to keep this illusion, near the beginning when there were only a few ops., they sent me down two men at different times who had broken their legs on parachute training on some quite different scheme. They hopped about in plaster and looked most convincing. One was a large Frenchman called Alexandre who liked to play the card game called 'barber' all day, when he wasn't at the pub. He survived the war and we met him in Bordeaux in 1956. The other was Guy, a young Belgian. I taught him to drive a car and he later went out to Belgium where he was arrested and shot. As he faced the firing squad, he asked them to take off his nice new leather jacket so that it should not be spoilt.

None of our people, of course, were in uniform when going out or coming in, but sometimes in the dark period the French were in uniform. Pierre-le-paysan was, but not looking very like an officer; it was rare for more than half his buttons to be done up. The high-ups who sometimes came to meet important new arrivals were always in uniform but they were rarely seen in the village. It was necessary to explain why sometimes Tony was at home for almost two weeks at a time. We did this at the pub. "They are going on with training," we said. Then we had to explain the presence of John in the uniform of the Wavy Navy (Royal Naval Volunteer Reserve) - that was liaison work; and of the frequent visits of pilots - more liaison work. And then there were the women. They were secretaries. Sometimes we had more secretaries than men for them to be secretaries to.

The pub was our great standby both for recreation and for security talk. The French took to darts and we frequently had matches against a village team. Once at closing time the score was even and we were pressed to come the next evening to settle it. We explained that the Frenchmen's sick-leave was over and they were returning to London the next day. The expected op. was cancelled, so we went to the pub next day after all and had to explain that their leave had been extended.

Another security difficulty was the little old woman who came round once a week collecting for the Red Cross. She always seemed to turn up at an inconvenient moment. Once, as she walked up the garden path, a Frenchman leant out of the window and fired his revolver into the air, "Just to see if it worked." I apologised to her as best I could but she was quite unmoved. "I know anything can happen in war," she said. My orders were only to explain without telling anyone anything!

There was also my cousin who came round with saving stamps. She told me after the war that she had noticed I had become very unfriendly and always stood with the door in my hand ready to shut it as soon as possible. She too, seemed to pick the wrong moments to call. Of course, my mother who lived close by, expected me to take the boys to tea with her frequently. It was difficult to explain to her that I couldn't leave the French to have tea by themselves because, so often at that moment, I was scrubbing out marks on a man's shirt.

To me the greatest strain was remembering not to mention the names of places. We would just say, "We are going to the village," "the Post," "the little town." The French knew that we were south of London and if we took them to Chichester or Brighton it was impossible for them not to know the name but otherwise they knew no names of local places. All signposts had been removed during the War. This was lucky because after a while the Gestapo sometimes asked them if they had passed through Major Bertram's house. If they said "Yes," the next question would be, "Where is it?" And that they could not answer.

There was no danger attached to my job but the Office gave me a little mini revolver that wouldn't have hurt a fly, even if I could have hit one. I suppose if anything had happened it would have made me feel safe, like wearing a tin hat in an air raid. They told me that in case of an invasion I was to take any French who happened to be in the house and drive west. As the Canadian troops stationed in the neighbourhood had already announced that in case of an invasion any civilian car on the road would be put in a ditch, I wouldn't have got far.

The only alarm I had was one night, at about one-thirty, I heard noises from the garage yard, so I went out and found a party of soldiers with a lorry just settling down for the night. I asked to speak to the Sergeant in charge and said firmly, "You can't stay here. It's important that the area is left clear." Luckily he believed me and obligingly moved off somewhere in the farm yard. What I should have done had he refused I don't know because I was expecting two car loads of French to arrive at about four that morning.

The boys were not really much of a risk and, from the security point of view, a good cover; no one would suspect that an ordinary household with two little boys, a cat and a dog would be doing anything important. As far as they were concerned the change-over of Frenchmen might have occurred at nine or ten at night instead of in the morning. Most of the conversation was in French which they had not even started to learn. There was one awkward occasion when Nicky came downstairs when he should have been asleep and the secret cupboard was open. A Frenchman quickly distracted him with an offer of chocolate and I whisked him back to bed - I doubt if he remembered it in the morning.

Our comparatively free use of petrol was another security problem and it was not helped by the Office giving me Admiralty petrol coupons when everyone knew that Tony was in the army and at the War Office. I always felt nervous getting petrol at local garages where we were known. Once, when I went to Chichester to shop, I was stopped and asked why I was using the car. I said I was going to see John Hunt the Security Officer and all was well.

Tony was ordered to report anyone in the neighbourhood who could not be accounted for. He reported one man and was told that he had already been reported five times and that there was nothing whatever against him. He always remained a mystery.

Of course MI-5 kept an eye on us though we didn't know it for certain at the time but a friend in the next village told me afterwards that a young niece who had never taken much notice of her before, started inviting herself for weekends - she was 'Something' at the War Office.

In the summer, as the incomers were arriving at Bignor from Tangmere, they often met the cows going to be milked. Tony always tried to make himself inconspicuous so as not to be noticed by the cowman.

I think the reason why we were able to do the job in a small village where everybody knew everybody was because, by lying freely, we never made a secret of anything. We always behaved as though we had nothing to hide. If an op. was put off and we had interesting people in the house, we sometimes asked the Armstrongs to dinner to meet them and then the talk would be of art and literature and the War would be forgotten for a few lovely hours.

Tony always hated all the deceit and subterfuge necessary and did not find lying at all easy. I'm afraid I was much better at it. We both realized, afterwards, what a strain all the secrecy had been.

6

Just before D-Day we were moved to a village near Bedford where a big house was requisitioned for us, a lovely Queen Anne house. The owner's wife and youngest daughter were allowed to stay there but we had the rest of the house with a small sitting room we kept for ourselves and a little enclosed 'master's garden' outside. When the War Office requisitioned it they told the local police and Air Raid Wardens never to go to the house without ringing up first. Consequently everyone knew we were 'hush-hush' and before we had been there a week they knew exactly what we were doing. The job changed utterly. I had a staff of six French soldiers. At least I was supposed to have, they never all materialised at once but there was a cook and his wife, a charming Algerian who flirted with the English charwoman - which caused me great embarrassment when I went up to see if the bedrooms were done properly - and one other Frenchman. The rest were always 'just coming'. There was plenty of room. Tony and I and the boys always had our own bedrooms. The boys went to Bedford School. The outlook was of a brickworks, instead of the South Downs.

There were a few memorable Frenchmen through the house. For instance, Monsieur Goyet who drew the cartoon at the beginning of this book. He sang comic songs looking slightly apprehensively at me and hoping *elle n'a pas compris*. There was a very young man who stood to attention whenever the Marseillaise was played on the radio, and that, in August 1944 was very frequently.

There were always other problems such as the occasion when the staff nearly mutinied because they had not been paid and a French Major came down, incredibly smart in his best uniform, and quelled them with promises of money by the next post. He went back the following day but the pay did not come. I kept up a continual battle with the cook against his black-market activities. There was the occasion when a sack of French money somehow fell out of an aeroplane and was scattered all over the countryside.

I was once allowed over to the aerodrome, lightly disguised as a French A.T.S. (Auxiliary Territorial Service; the equivalent in France - Service des femmes dans l'armée de terre) and went in a Lysander - a most uncomfortable machine that went crab-wise like a tiresome horse - to the field where they practised night landings and watched Tony and one of the pilots try the new parcel-pickup. This entailed the pilot flying down to about six feet off the ground while Tony fished for a parcel on a string between two posts with a hook on the end of a rod that hung down from the Lysander. It was a very tricky operation and was only used in France a few times. Tony tried to persuade those in charge to let him try the first time but this was refused.

There was now comfort and space and leisure but the old love and intimacy was gone.

There was a nice incident when Tony arrived from London with the high-up in charge of finance. He knew little or nothing of what we were doing. He explained to me that I must always keep the accounts in double-entry but failed to tell me what he meant by that. I thought I just had to put everything down twice. On the way down he asked Tony what arrangement had been made about fruit and vegetables from the garden. Tony explained that we were buying them from the gardener at market prices. "You

73

won't give them asparagus or peaches or things like that, will you," he said. "Oh no, sir," said Tony, "Except in the case of schedule A." "Yes, of course," said the bewildered high-up. After that I headed all my accounts 'Schedule A'. He inspected the store-room that took the place of the secret cupboard at Bignor. Tony was working so I showed him the coshes, tooth brushes, tablets of poison etc.

"I hope you make them sign for everything they take," he said.

"I'm sure my husband sees to that," I lied. He went away satisfied.

Then came the Liberation of France and there were no French with us to celebrate and our job came to an end. The boys and I went back to Bignor and Tony followed shortly to write the official history of the job.

Sometime in the winter of 1944-5, Monsieur Soustelle gave a lunch for me in London and presented me with a silver cigarette case with a gold Croix de Lorraine on it. After I gave up smoking I had it made into a powder compact.

There was also a farewell party at the Cottage at Tangmere for pilots, Conducting Officers, drivers, a few high-ups and me. We played silly games, sang the old songs and drank too much - a good party.

When saying goodbye to the 'Hullabaloos' as they left for Tangmere, I often said, "I'll see you after the war in Paris," but I never thought I would. Immediately after the war Tony got a job with the British Council in Paris and we did see a great many of our friends. Some by appointment - Tony knew their real names - some accidentally in the street, in the Metro, in cafes.

We went to a Requiem Mass in the Sacré-Coeur for the members of Marie Madeleine's réseau - five hundred killed from that one réseau. Marie Madeleine, you will remember was the mistress of disguise who told me of the tortures.

Two months before the presentation of the Lysander to the French Air Ministry, mentioned by Tony in his introduction, he had been invested with the Légion d'Honneur and Croix de Guerre avec Palme.

The kaleidoscope of the job still goes through my head and I shall never forget our 'Hullabaloos', their courage, their cheerfulness. their generosity and their love. I fear that I may have jumbled things up and distorted some things a little; it is all so long ago. All the same the thought of France still makes me feel sick with anxiety and whenever I hear the Marseillaise again, I know I shall cry.

FOOTNOTE

The population of Bignor has dropped by almost a third since the 1940's. Many of those who might have wondered what was going on, but did not ask questions, have died or moved away. There are many new faces. The village itself, however, has remained largely unchanged. Tangmere aerodrome is no more. Whilst there remains only the deserted control tower and a few buildings, there is a splendid Museum of Military Aviation, that houses much information on the role of the Lysander in those heroic days.

Walking on the Downs above Bignor on a warm, still day in summer or on a night made cold and sharp by moonlight, it is easy to picture those days of courage, fear and selfless determination.

The many people who heard her story over the years felt privileged to have known Barbara Bertram and proud of the part she played.